THE LOGIC OF AMERICAN POLITICS IN WARTIME

LESSONS FROM THE BUSH ADMINISTRATION

A Supplement to
The Logic of American Politics

Gary C. Jacobson and Samuel Kernell
University of California,
San Diego

CQ PRESS

A Division of Congressional Quarterly Inc.
Washington, D.C.

CQ Press
1255 22nd St., N.W., Suite 400
Washington, D.C. 20037

Phone, 202-729-1900
Toll-free, 1-866-4CQ-PRESS (1-866-427-7737)

www.cqpress.com

♾ The paper used in this publication exceeds the requirements of the American National Standard for Information Sciences—Permanence of Paper for Printed Library Materials, ANSI Z39.48-1992.

Cover design: Michael Pottman
Composition: Auburn Associates, Inc., Baltimore, Maryland

Image credits: cover, 8, 12, 22, 36, 40, 41, AP/Wide World Photos; 13, *CQ Weekly*/Scott J. Ferrell; 2, 24, 38, 42, Reuters; 10, Christopher Weyant, *The Hill;* 31, WNYT TV

Printed and bound in the United States of America

07   06   05   04   5   4   3   2

ISBN: 1-56802-863-6

CONTENTS

THE LOGIC OF AMERICAN POLITICS IN WARTIME

Lessons from the Bush Administration

The Public

The terrorist attacks of September 11, 2001, on New York City and Washington, D.C., put the United States on a war footing. The government's initial focus on strengthening homeland security against further terrorist threats was quickly followed by an American-led invasion of Afghanistan, whose Taliban government had refused to turn over Osama bin Ladin and other al Qaeda leaders responsible for orchestrating the assaults. Saddam Hussein's repressive Iraqi regime became the next target, as the George W. Bush administration accused it of aiding al Qaeda and secretly producing weapons of mass destruction (biological, chemical, and nuclear). The agreement that ended the 1991 Gulf war had forbidden Iraq to have such weapons, and the administration argued that Hussein, if not removed, would use them to threaten Iraq's neighbors or to arm terrorists bent on destroying the United States and its allies. Despite lack of support from the United Nations and vocal opposition by other major powers—including China, France, Germany, and Russia—U.S. and British military forces invaded Iraq on March 20, 2003. By April 14 they had toppled Hussein's regime and were in control of Iraq's major cities, including its capital, Baghdad.

The rapid military successes in Afghanistan and Iraq did not promise an equally rapid restoration of peace. Bin Laden and Hussein, along with other prominent leaders of al Qaeda and Iraq's former regime, remained at large. Conflicting Iraqi groups, some openly hostile to the U.S. occupation, struggled to fill the power vacuum left by Hussein's fall. The American military forces faced the difficult task of

1

President Bush's nationally televised address on March 17, 2003, announcing and justifying war with Iraq drew an audience of seventy-three million viewers, a figure exceeded in recent years only by the Super Bowl and Bush's address after 9/11. Immediately following the broadcast, national polls recorded a surge in the public's support for war.

reestablishing order while trying to restore essential services and set up a new government. Meanwhile, Syria and Iran came under scrutiny as possible refuges for terrorists or Hussein's fleeing henchmen. And North Korea began expanding its nuclear weapons program, provoking a potentially dangerous confrontation in Asia.

Although involved in overseas military action almost continuously since the end of the cold war (*Logic*, 244, Figure 7-2), the United States took on the characteristics of a country at war only after the deadly September 11 attacks on American soil. War changes the strategic environment of American politics. It recasts the public agenda, raising the salience of some issues while relegating others to the back burner. It changes the way ordinary citizens think about leaders and policies and, therefore, affects the preferences people express in public opinion polls and in the voting booth. In wartime, the president's constitutional role as commander in chief of the armed forces and symbolic role as national leader inspire unusual deference from other political leaders. The need for coordination and speed in responding collectively to imminent threats mandates a reduction in transaction costs at the expense of increasing conformity costs (*Logic,* 13). A state of war thus greatly strengthens the White House in its dealings with the other institutions of government—Congress, the administrative agencies, and the courts. It also alters power relationships among and within these institutions. Exactly how remains an open question, decided in the end by the assertiveness and skill of institutional leaders and the extent to which their policy preferences agree or differ. A state of war does not, however, resolve basic political or institutional conflicts, dampen political ambitions, or guarantee that presidents will get what they wanted from other participants in government, particularly in policy domains remote from national defense. In short, wartime creates opportunities for presidents to shift the balance of power in their favor, but their success or failure depends on politics. The events of September 11 and their aftermath radically altered the strategic terrain of American politics, but they did not alter its fundamental logic.

In this supplement to *The Logic of American Politics,* we examine various aspects of wartime politics during the Bush administration that illuminate important features of the American political system discussed at greater length in the main text. We also consider how politicians responded strategically to the new challenges and opportunities posed by the post–September 11 political environment. Since the most consequential transactions in Washington occurred among elected officeholders and others—such as the news media, which also, for their own reasons, pay close attention to the public—we begin our investigation into the effects of the wartime environment by examining the responses of the ultimate delegators—the American public. We turn first to public opinion and then to an examination of how those opinions translated into votes in the 2002 congressional elections.

Public Opinion

September 11 provoked an unprecedented upsurge of patriotic support for American leaders and institutions, particularly President Bush. Also, military action in Afghanistan in pursuit of al Qaeda enjoyed nearly unanimous public support (*Logic,* 375–376, 380–381). After the Taliban fell and the terrorist bases in Afghanistan were dismantled, Bush's overall level of approval declined, but only gradually; it was still near 60 percent before the onset of the Iraq war spurred

Figure 1.   President Bush's Job Performance Ratings in Wartime

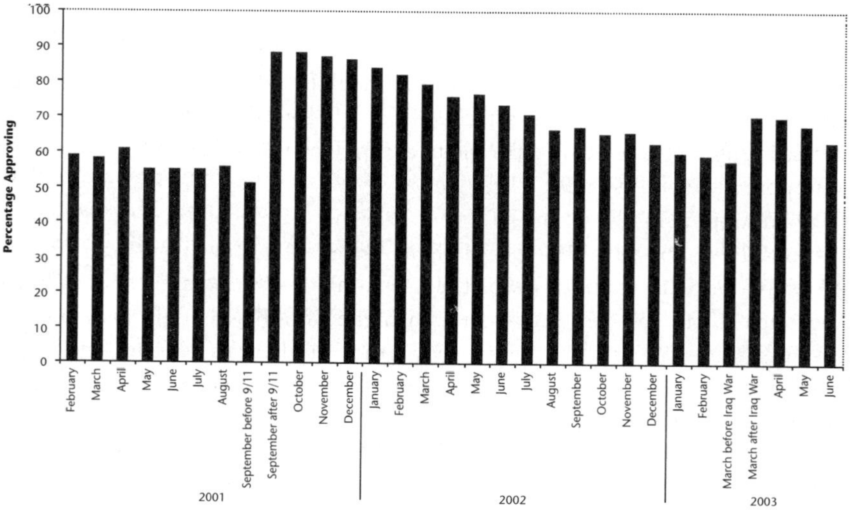

Source: Monthly averages of Gallup polls at www.pollingreport.com

another, more modest patriotic rally (Figure 1). Bush's leadership in response to the terrorist attacks had settled most lingering doubts about the legitimacy of his presidency (left in question by the controversial Florida vote count) and had solidified his public image as a strong and decisive leader.

The attack on Afghanistan was an easy sell; backing for military action aimed at Bin Laden's network and its Taliban protectors was overwhelming and bipartisan.[1] Most Americans, convinced by the administration's claims that Saddam Hussein was allied with al Qaeda and hiding weapons of mass destruction, also approved the use of military force to drive him from power in Iraq. But prior to the war, large majorities preferred a diplomatic solution if at all possible, and support for military action was much lower if it were to be taken without strong international support. Most wanted to allow the United Nation's weapons inspectors all the time they needed to complete their investigations before initiating war.[2] No small part of the public seemed to be looking to America's European allies and the UN weapons inspectors to provide independent confirmation of the Bush administration's arguments for the necessity of war with Iraq before giving it their complete backing— a noteworthy example of principals using third parties to monitor their agents (*Logic,* 21).

Although this confirmation was not forthcoming, the administration's opinion leadership nonetheless prevailed. This is not surprising, for the president is the preeminent opinion leader on foreign affairs (*Logic,* 380). Some Democratic leaders and media commentators did express doubts about Hussein's personal involvement in September 11 and argued that the UN inspections could deal with the threat posed by whatever weapons of mass destruction Iraq actually possessed. But when the administration, led by the popular president and the even more popular secretary of state, Colin Powell, argued the case against Hussein's regime, the public tended to resolve its doubts in the administration's favor.[3] The very real threat revealed by the attacks of September 11 and the administration's success in Afghanistan inclined people to accept its analysis of the Iraqi threat and to support a preemptive war.

Public support for invading Iraq grew after the war began (if only out of support for U.S. troops once they were in harm's way) and grew again after the military phase was successfully completed. But it always varied substantially across subgroups (*Logic,* 381–385). It was much higher among Republicans, conservatives, men, and whites than it was among Democrats, liberals, women, and African Americans (Table 1). As would be expected, the gaps between these groups narrowed somewhat as overall support grew, but they remained large. On all questions regarding Iraq, components of the president's electoral coalition were notably more willing to accept his arguments and follow his lead (*Logic,* 460). The Iraq war did not restore the extraordinary national unity inspired by September 11.

Indeed, most Americans were willing to defer to Bush's judgement and accept his leadership on war policies, but popular deference did not extend to his domestic policies. During the first five months of 2003, approval of his performance on the economy remained about 18 points below his overall rating and 29 points below his approval rating on terrorism. Most polls taken in April and May found less than half the public endorsing his performance on this front. The domain-specific nature of presidential approval is strikingly confirmed in Figure 2, which

Table 1. Public Support for a War in Iraq

	Before Iraq war [a]	During Iraq war	After Iraq war [b]
All respondents	55	72	77
Republicans	75	93	95
Conservatives	68	84	88
Men	59	78	82
Whites	58	78	81
Moderates	52	70	78
Women	51	66	72
Independents	50	66	n.a.
Democrats	39	53	65
Liberals	36	44	63
African Americans	37	29	49

[a] Gallup polls conducted December 2002–January 2003, and March 22–24, 2003, reported at www.gallup.com

[b] Washington Post/ABC News poll conducted April 6, 2003, reported at www.washingtonpost.com/wp~srv/politics/polls/vault/stories/data040703.htm.

Figure 2. Approval of President Bush's Job Performance across Policy Domains

Do you approve or disapprove of the way Bush is handling:

The U.S. campaign against terrorism	79	19	2
The situation in Iraq	75	22	3
Homeland security	74	23	3
The situation with North Korea	61	27	12
Education	59	34	7
The situation between Israel and the Palestinians	54	33	13
The economy	52	45	3
Taxes	50	46	4
Social Security	49	38	13
The environment	49	40	11
Prescription drug benefits for the elderly	44	40	16
The federal budget	43	50	7
Cost, availability, and coverage of health insurance	34	57	9

0% 10% 20% 30% 40% 50% 60% 70% 80% 90% 100%

■ Approve   ☐ Disapprove   ☐ No Opinion

Source: Washington Post/ABC News poll, at www.washingtonpost.com/wp-dyn/articles/A1938–2003May1.html.

shows Bush's approval ratings in thirteen issue areas in a poll taken shortly after the military victory in Iraq. In general he won high approval ratings in defense and foreign policy areas but considerably lower ratings in domestic policy areas. Even within these broad categories, however, differences are quite large. Aggregate public opinion displays a nuanced evaluation of the president's performance; the popular success of his leadership in the Iraq war did not automatically extend to his performance on domestic policy issues.

Popular approval is thought to be an important resource presidents can draw on to help persuade other politicians to support their policies. But approval in one policy domain does not necessarily translate into approval in other domains (Figure 2). Although the president's aggressive foreign policy won broad public support, especially when it appeared to be successful (with the defeat of the Taliban and the fall of Baghdad), popular support for his domestic policies did not increase. The Bush administration's positions on energy development, taxes, abortion, prescription drug benefits, and Social Security did not become more popular after September 11 or after the Iraq war than they had been before.[4]

The public's tepid response to the president's proposed tax cut, the third in his first three years in office, provides a good example. Normally, voters warm up to tax cuts with little prompting. But with the federal budget deficit back again and threatening to grow much larger as the war's costs mounted, most Americans seemed to prefer paying down the budget deficit to cutting taxes. In a poll taken in January 2003, right after President Bush used his nationally televised State of the Union address to lobby for a $726 billion tax cut, 36 percent of respondents preferred the tax cut, whereas 56 percent opted for debt reduction. Three months later and with the Iraq war just concluding, support for the tax cut had fallen to 32 percent. With a vote on the tax bill pending in May and victory uncertain despite Republican control of both the House and the Senate, Bush campaigned around the country in an effort to build a fire under Congress to support the entire package. The public remained largely unmoved; when the question was repeated in a mid-May poll, only 31 percent endorsed the tax cut.[5] Bush proved unable to convert popular acclaim for his wartime leadership into support for this centerpiece of his domestic agenda. As a result, Bush's domestic proposals did not enjoy the same smooth sailing in Congress as his foreign and defense policies.

The 2002 Midterm Elections

The president might have expected to have his way with Congress after the 2002 midterm elections, which increased the Republican House majority to 229 and restored the Republican Senate majority, lost when Senator James Jeffords left the Republican Party in 2001 (*Logic*, 187–188; the election results are summarized in Table 2). Bush took an active role in the campaign and earned considerable credit for a party victory against the historical grain (since the Civil War, only twice before— 1934 and 1998—had the president's party picked up House seats at midterm).

September 11 and its aftermath proved enormously helpful to the Republicans in this election. Not only did Bush's leadership in the war on terrorism keep his approval ratings high, which always helps a president's party at midterm, but it also changed the focus of national politics from domestic issues, where Democrats enjoyed a popular edge, to national defense, a Republican strength. Democrats played into Republicans' hands by holding up legislation establishing the Department of Homeland Security in a dispute with the administration over job protection for federal workers in the new department, which the president and his allies took as license for attacking Democrats as indifferent to the terrorist threat. The

Table 2. Membership Changes in the 2002 Midterm Elections

	Republicans	Democrats	Independents	Vacant
House of Representatives				
Elected in 2000	221	212	2	
At the time of the 2002 election	223	208	1	3
Elected in 2002	229	205	1	
Senate				
After the 2000 election	50	50		
At the time of the 2002 election	49	49	1	1
After the 2002 election	51	48	1	

Source: Compiled by authors.

President Bush targeted Georgia in a big way during the 2002 midterm elections. His three major campaign and fund-raising trips paid off handsomely, as Sonny Perdue (left) and Saxby Chambliss (right) took the governorship and a Senate seat, respectively, away from Democratic incumbents.

focus on terrorism also helped the president and his party avoid damage from financial scandals involving major Bush campaign contributors, notably those associated with Enron, the bankrupt energy giant, and it provided an excuse for the feeble national economy and return of large federal budget deficits. The shift from "domestic economy" to "national security" campaign themes (*Logic,* 405–407) was a godsend to Republican candidates, framing the choice in terms much more favorable to their cause.

President Bush's near-universal approval among Republicans guaranteed him receptive audiences wherever he traveled to raise campaign funds for his party's House and Senate candidates. Although the war in Afghanistan delayed the start of the fund-raising season, by election day Bush had headlined seventy-four different events to the benefit of fifty-three candidates. Counting soft money contributions (*Logic,* 414), he raised more than $193 million, eclipsing by about 20 percent President Bill Clinton's record-setting fund-raising take in 2000 (Table 3; *Logic,* 464–465). Abundant cash, combined with Bush's frenzied last-minute campaigning in competitive states and the national party's effective grassroots drives to get out the vote, proved essential to Republican victories in several tight Senate races (on the importance of organized voter mobilization, see *Logic,* 397–398). For the most part, however, the 2002 elections reiterated the close partisan balance and sharp ideological and cultural divisions in the United States that were revealed so clearly by the 2000 elections (*Logic,* 391, 460–462). Indeed, the Republican gains in the House were entirely explainable by the party's successful gerrymandering

Table 3. President Bush's Fund-raising Record in the 2002 Midterm Elections

Recipient	Number of candidates	Number of events	$ Total	$ Per candidate
Senate incumbents	8	7	5,950,000	743,750.00
Senate challengers	8	9	9,133,332	1,141,666.50
Senate open	4	4	3,850,000	962,500.00
House incumbents	8	6	3,475,833	434,479.12
House challengers	5	3	1,563,333	312,666.60
Governor incumbents	5	6	6,705,000	1,341,000.00
Governor challengers	13	12	21,766,666	1,674,358.90
Governor open	1	1	1,800,000	1,800,000.00
Jeb Bush	1	1	500,000	500,000.00
Florida Repub Party		4	6,000,000	
State/local party		13	12,540,832	
RNC/RCCC		1	23,900,000	
RNC		1	33,000,000	
NRSC/NRCC		2	50,000,000	
NRSC		2	10,250,000	
RGA		1	3,000,000	
Other organizations		1	400,000	
Total	53	74	193,834,996	

Source: Mark Knoller, CBS News.

(*Logic,* 193) in the decennial redistricting that occurred between 2000 and 2002.[6] Nonetheless, President Bush was widely credited with a bold and successful strategy that effectively translated the war on terrorism and his own public standing into a solid Republican victory. With both houses of Congress in grateful Republican hands, prospects for the president's agenda looked bright.

Congress

Wartime strengthens the president at the expense of Congress. Consistent with the Framers' design (*Logic,* 240–241), the Constitution allows quick and energetic executive action in times of national crisis. Moreover, public support for presidents is highest in such moments, so opposition to presidential demands carries unusually high political risks. President Bush, like his predecessors, did not hesitate to use this institutional advantage to expand his control over policy and programs.

Congress quickly complied, by huge majorities, with the president's request for legislation to deal with the crisis provoked by the attacks of September 11. Only a single member of Congress voted against the joint resolution passed on September 14 authorizing the president "to use all necessary and appropriate force against the nations, organizations, or people that he determines planned, authorized, committed, or aided the terrorist attacks on the United States that occurred September 11, 2001" (PL 107-46). A week later, the airline relief bill (PL 107-42) passed overwhelmingly, followed a short time later by the Patriot Act, which relaxed restrictions on surveillance and otherwise strengthened the government's capacity to ferret out terrorists and seize their assets.[7] The president also got his way on more controversial issues, for example, first successfully resisting the push in Congress to replace the White House Office of Homeland Security with a full cabinet-level Department of Homeland Security (*Logic*, 316), and then, months later, after a 180-degree turn to the idea, getting Congress to establish the department under rules that maximized the president's "management flexibility." (The organization of this department is discussed in the next section.)

The most consequential and instructive example of the president's advantage in conducting foreign policy during moments of crisis came in early October when the Democratic-controlled Senate basically capitulated to the administration's demand for blanket authority to decide if and when the nation would invade Iraq. Initially, President Bush and Vice President Dick Cheney asserted that the president needed no new authority from Congress. But when some normally loyal sup-

porters among congressional Republicans joined in criticizing the president's uni-lateral—some critics said "imperial"—posture, the White House relented and sent a draft resolution to Congress that authorized force "to restore international peace and security to the region." This language did not satisfy congressional skeptics, and almost immediately committees in both chambers went to work drafting al-ternative legislation. A bipartisan resolution drafted by the chair and ranking Re-publican member of the Senate Foreign Relations Committee would have re-quired the president to get a United Nations resolution authorizing force before initiating war unless he were prepared to state that the threat to America was "so grave" that the nation had to take immediate action. But with the midterm con-gressional elections less than a month away and Bush delivering campaign speeches claiming that certain congressional Democrats "were not interested in the security of the American people," House Democratic leader and aspiring pres-idential contender Dick Gephardt sought political cover for himself and his party by negotiating a compromise resolution with the president.[8]

The new language revealed just how strong a hand the president was playing. It allowed him to commit American forces "as he determines to be necessary and appropriate" to counter "the continuing threat posed by Iraq," and to enforce "all relevant" United Nations Security Council resolutions concerning Iraq from the 1991 war. The congressional resolution limited military action to Iraq, although it did require the president to declare that international diplomacy was failing to bring Iraq into compliance with existing UN resolutions before taking military ac-tion. Finally, with language that explicitly proclaimed the resolution's provisions to be in compliance with the War Powers Act (*Logic*, 243), it obliged the president to confer with Congress within sixty days of the beginning of hostilities. The res-olution passed the House easily, and over the strident objections of a group of Senate Democrats who sought unsuccessfully to amend it, passed the Senate by 77 to 23.[9] Reflecting the perspective of someone who had just been steamrolled, Senator Richard Durbin (D-Ill.) proclaimed the resolution to be nothing less than "the largest grant of presidential authority ever given by a Congress."[10]

As the nation went to war, Congress continued to give the president a compar-atively free rein in matters related to defense. Bush had asked that he be given total discretion in deciding how to spend $60 billion of the $78.5 billion supplemental appropriation for the Iraq war. He had already been given such discretion over the $40 billion appropriated in response to September 11, and his secretary of defense, Donald Rumsfeld, had said flatly that "whatever is put forward by the Congress by way of money will be expended in a way that the president decides it should be ex-pended."[11] Bush was by no means the first president to demand a blank check, but Congress usually has kept a tight fist on the purse strings even in wartime, for control over funds is at the heart of its institutional power. This time Congress raised a partial defense of its power of the purse. The House voted for $25.4 bil-lion in discretionary funds, the Senate $11 billion, and the conference committee

On October 3, 2002, Senator Robert Byrd spoke out against the resolution granting President Bush unprecedented power, "How have we gotten to this low point in the history of Congress? Are we too feeble to resist the demands of a president who is determined to bend the collective will of Congress to his will—a president who is changing the conventional understanding of the term 'self-defense'?"

compromised at $15.7 billion.[12] The president "lost" only because he had asked for so much; in fact, he was, by historical standards, remarkably successful in wresting financial authority from its congressional guardians.

On issues having little or nothing to do with national security, however, neither wartime deference nor Republican majorities in both houses of Congress guaranteed presidential success. Although President Bush argued forcefully that his plan, defeated in the previous Democratic-controlled Senate, to open the Arctic National Wildlife Refuge on the north coast of Alaska to oil exploration was critical to America's "energy independence" from Mideast oil, the provision was stripped from the energy bill by a 52–48 vote in the Senate, with eight Republicans joining the opposition. His proposal to slash taxes by $726 billion, the administration's chosen instrument for jump-starting the stagnant economy, was blocked in the Senate, where two moderate Republicans, fearing huge budget deficits, would supply the votes necessary for a tax cut only if it were reduced to $350 billion. The final figure, enacted in late May 2003, was $330 billion, the third (and largest) tax cut Bush had successfully promoted during his first three years in office.[13]

Bush got even this more limited tax cut only because the Senate's rules forbid filibusters (*Logic,* 228–229) on budget resolutions, allowing the bill to be enacted

Secretary of Defense Donald Rumsfeld converses with Senate Democrats during a defense legislation hearing intermission. Rumsfeld followed the Bush administration's standard and mostly successful script of asking for a lot and taking (and taking credit for) whatever Congress agreed to give.

by a simple majority vote. On other issues, Senate Democrats were in a position to veto actions via filibuster when they remained united. They continued to block the appointment of two conservatives to the federal bench as the Iraq war wound down, with more filibusters threatened. In dealing with Congress, presidential power in wartime is still no more than the power to persuade members that doing the president's bidding will ultimately benefit them politically. If they are not persuaded, if their constituents are hostile or indifferent to the president's agenda, or if they simply doubt the wisdom of the president's proposals, they remain free to assert their independence. Indeed, members of Congress, compelled by wartime to give extraordinary deference to the president's demands on defense matters, may look for ways to assert themselves on other issues to reclaim their institutional authority.

It is no accident that all the president's setbacks discussed here occurred in the Senate. The tight control the Republican leadership has exercised over the House since 1995 (*Logic*, 210) became even tighter in the 108th Congress (2003–2004). The 2002 elections left the Republican House delegation more homogeneously conservative than ever, and only Democrats squawked when Republican leaders made heavy use of such devices as "closed rules" (*Logic*, 227) to dominate the legislative process.[14] The Senate's rules give the minority much more opportunity to obstruct the majority, through filibuster or the threat of filibuster as well as by

Real War Heroes Eat Pork

Dave Barry

It is time to sing about some unsung heroes of the recent war in Iraq. These heroes were not, personally, in Iraq, but they were serving in a place that is just as foreign and threatening to the average American: The United States Senate.

Our story begins back in March. The war had started, and the Bush administration asked Congress for an emergency appropriation of $75 billion to pay for it. The House of Representatives, showing a disappointing lack of vision, basically just approved the money.

But not the Senate. No sir. Because the United States Senate is not a bunch of "yes-persons" who "rubber-stamp" every bill that comes down the pike. And so the Senate, exercising its constitutional responsibility, took a hard look at the bill to pay for the war in Iraq, and discovered a shocking omission: There was nothing in there about sea lampreys.

In case you are unfamiliar with national security, I should explain that sea lampreys are nasty parasite fish that latch on to other fish and suck their blood. The only known way to stop them is to equip all the other fish with tiny waterproof crucifixes.

But seriously, lampreys are a problem, and so Sen. Patrick Leahy of Vermont decided that the war-funding bill should include $500,000 to control lampreys in Lake Champlain, which is right next to Vermont and therefore very strategic.

The sea-lamprey effort was only one of more than $600 million worth of new items that various senators, both Republican and Democrat, wanted to insert into the war bill. These items included: feed subsidies for catfish farmers; $50 million for the shipbuilding industry; $3.3 million to repair a dam in (surprise!) Vermont; $10 million for a research station at the South Pole; $98 million for an agricultural research facility in Iowa; a provision that would have allowed senators to send postcards to more voters at taxpayers' expense; and another provision that would have allowed wild Alaskan salmon to be labeled "organic."

According to *The New York Times,* many of these extra items were slipped into the bill at the last minute by the chairman of the Senate Appropriations Committee, Sen. Ted Stevens (R-OINK), who represents Alaska, which is the largest state, which is good, because that way it has room for all the taxpayer money that old Ted ships there. The

less dramatic means (*Logic,* 215–216, 228). They also make it easier for moderate Republicans to resist the demands of party leaders. Hence, while the House obediently followed the president's lead on domestic as well as foreign policy issues, the Senate did not (see the excerpt from the *New York Times,* "Behind Clashes, Two Chambers That Don't Understand Each Other").

Times said that "many senators never realized" that these items had been stuck into the war bill they approved. (Members of Congress rarely read the bills they vote on; they're too busy serving the public.)

When word got out about the extra projects, Sen. John McCain, a big spoilsport about this kind of thing, raised a stink. He said that even if these projects were worthwhile, they had no business being in the war bill. Or, as he put it, "the sea lamprey does not, in my opinion, pose a clear and present danger to our national security." Various House members also criticized the senators for using a national emergency to avoid normal legislative scrutiny and make taxpayers pay for flagrant pork, although, to their credit, none of them pointed out that Flagrant Pork would be a good name for a rock band.

This criticism really got up the dander of the senators who pushed to have the pork. . . I mean, the additional items, put into the war bill. Sen. Arlen Specter of Pennsylvania claimed that sending out taxpayer-financed postcards to announce his public meetings was—he actually said this—"directly related to the war effort" because "meeting with the people of Pennsylvania is an important part of our job, including informing them of the war effort."

Did I mention that Arlen is running for re-election? No? Well, it's probably irrelevant.

Anyway, House leaders were really upset about the extra items in the war bill, and demanded that the Senate remove them. This made Sen. Stevens so mad that, according to the Associated Press, he told reporters: "I'm just sorry we repealed the law on dueling."

On behalf of the taxpayers, let me say: We're sorry, too, Sen. Stevens! If you want to bring dueling back, the pistols are on us!

Anyway, in the end, the Senate caved, and most of the extra items were yanked from the bill. For now, the voters of Pennsylvania remain dangerously uninformed about the war, and the fish of Vermont remain tragically vulnerable to terrorist lampreys. So, this time at least, these bold senators failed in their mission. But the point is, darn it, they had the courage to try. And I'm sure that, one day, they'll try again: They'll see their chance, and they'll make their move, swimming swiftly up to their prey and fastening their suckers onto the. . .

No, wait, sorry. I'm thinking of the lampreys.

Source: Copyright 2003, Tribune Media Services. Reprinted with permission.

The Senate was also more inclined to engage in politics as usual, even on defense legislation. The House passed the $78.5 billion supplemental spending measure to cover the cost of the Iraq war without adding any members' pet projects, but the Senate added $675 million in pork barrel spending (later reduced to $355 million in conference). Afterward, according to one experienced observer, "the level of rage House Republicans feel toward the Senate Republican leadership is high. They saw the supplemental [appropriation] being for the war. The Senate behaved in a completely different fashion"[15] (see sidebar for Dave Barry's amusing treatment of these events). House Republicans were also angered by the Senate Republicans' inability to deliver more on Bush's tax cut proposal. Intra-branch squabbling, even among legislators sharing a party label with a popular wartime president, underlines the continuing effectiveness of James Madison's institutional machinery for pitting ambition against ambition (*Logic,* 63).

Congress, then, gave wide latitude to the administration on defense- and war-related matters, but on domestic issues, politics as usual reigned. This is not surprising when we remember that the public was much more strongly supportive of the president on the former than on the latter. Congressional Democrats in particular had little reason to back the president's tax, energy, and budget proposals because most of the people who had voted for them did not. The administration naturally tried to use the political capital it earned through its successes on the battlefield in Afghanistan and then in Iraq to further its entire agenda, but it was much more successful in rallying its core Republican supporters than in bringing other Americans on board.

The administration also sought to extend the president's broad commander-in-chief authority to other executive functions, renewing the struggle with Congress for control of the bureaucracy that has been part of American politics since the first Congress.

Behind Clashes,
Two Chambers That Don't Understand Each Other

Carl Hulse

WASHINGTON, May 11—Forget Republicans and Democrats. The lawmakers who seem least to understand each other are senators and representatives—no matter the party.

Senators feel maligned and misunderstood by House members who do not grasp the complexities of the upper chamber. "They never really understand until some of them come over here and become good senators," said Senator Ted Stevens, Republican of Alaska.

On the other side of the Capitol Rotunda, Speaker J. Dennis Hastert of Illinois complained the other day that he was tired of trying to fit the House to the Senate.

Representative Tom DeLay of Texas, the House majority leader, said he realized the Senate was not going away, though he sounded as if he wished it would.

Even with one-party control, the vast differences in the way the House and the Senate operate make policy blowups inevitable. Throughout history, the House and the Senate have clashed. But lately those clashes have been frequent—and loud.

The House is insisting on oil drilling in Alaska; the Senate has rejected the idea. The Senate blocked a Bush administration proposal to give public money to religious groups, compelling the House to go along. The House is ready to advance a Medicare overhaul; the Senate is taking it slower. And the latest dispute was on Friday. House Republicans pushed through a tax-cut package substantially at odds in size and content with the measure emerging in the Senate, setting up a nasty negotiation to reconcile the two.

"We expedite, they obstruct," a top House Republican aide said.

While differences in policy goals certainly exist, the problem can often be found in the very nature of the institutions. House rules severely restrain the power of the opposition, giving Mr. Hastert and Mr. DeLay iron-fisted control so they can—and do—rapidly ram through almost anything they want.

In the Senate, every member wields tremendous power through the ability to put blind "holds" on legislation, raise procedural obstacles on the floor and generally gum things up. That makes the Senate a place where the majority does not always rule.

The House leadership uses a Rules Committee to limit debate; the Senate routinely engages in interminable debates without limits.

"It is an entirely different legislative body from the House, literally," said Senator Saxby Chambliss, Republican of Georgia and a recent arrival from the House who is still adjusting to the style of business.

The differences are as old as the Constitution. But even the new Senate majority leader, Bill Frist of Tennessee, seemed taken aback by the House response after he made a side deal to pass a budget recently. Given that two Republicans were threatening to bolt from his 51–49 majority, Dr. Frist felt that he did not have much choice. But House leaders were outraged.

"Bill Frist is learning what it is to be the leader of a majority with 51 votes," said the Senate Democratic leader, Tom Daschle, who has ample experience in this area. "You have to earn that majority every day with every bill and every amendment and every vote. That learning process can be excruciating."

The power of the individual in the Senate was on vivid display again last week as Senator Olympia J. Snowe, Republican of Maine, single-handedly forced the Finance Committee to compromise on a tax-cutting plan that raised some taxes to pay for tax cuts elsewhere. That idea did not go down well in the House.

"I think the Capitol Police better check to see if someone's slipped something into the water over there," said Representative Mark Foley, Republican of Florida, adding that the Senate tax-writers were "not acting like Republicans."

Indeed. They were acting like senators.

"It is frustrating to them that we can't always perform as the House Republicans do," said Senator Jon Kyl, Republican of Arizona, a former House member. "I understand that frustration. But it is the nature of the Senate."

The framers of the Constitution envisioned the Senate as a legislative bulwark against the more populist House, and Washington famously and perhaps apocryphally described it to Jefferson as the saucer to "cool" the passions of the House members.

To Al Swift, a lobbyist and former Democratic representative from Washington who often poked fun at the stodginess of the Senate, that formulation was a huge mistake. "I think you can make an awfully good argument that the Senate is the least democratic democratic institution on the face of the earth," Mr. Swift said. "You are able to prevent the majority from working its will well beyond anything that should be allowed."

In the early years of the nation, the House was where the action was, with the Senate a sleepy chamber caught up in confirmations. The Senate historian Richard A. Baker said that balance of power changed with the rising emphasis on slavery issues in the 19th century. With the Senate split between slave states and free states, politicians quickly realized that one lawmaker in the Senate could wield significant power.

"That is where the political talent of the nation went, where a single member could make a difference if only to stand up and say no," Mr. Baker said.

Tension between the House and the Senate even when both are controlled by the same party is hardly new. Some House Republicans are still angry at the Senate for what they contend was a perfunctory trial of the impeachment case against President Bill Clinton in 1999 and for slighting the Republican "Contract with America" in 1995. House Democrats said they were left holding the bag in 1993 when they passed a new energy tax as part of Mr. Clinton's economic plan only to see it jettisoned by Senate Democrats.

Because Senators represent entire states, they often are less ideological and unyielding than House members, who are often elected from safe partisan districts and can afford to be less willing to compromise.

Things could well get worse before they get better in the current Congress, with coming negotiations over the tax bill, drug coverage under Medicare, energy policy and the usual list of spending measures.

But not everyone is complaining. Senator Lindsey Graham, a South Carolina Republican, said he was quickly discovering the joys of the Senate after his days as one of 435 members of the House.

"I like it over here," Mr. Graham said. "One person or a couple of people really do matter."

Bureaucratic Politics

The terrorist attacks of September 11 put the issue of homeland security at the top of the political agenda. President Bush's initial response was an executive order establishing a White House Office of Homeland Security, to be headed by former Pennsylvania governor Tom Ridge and charged with coordinating domestic preparedness and counterterrorism among some fifty federal agencies. As knowledgeable people in Congress and elsewhere predicted at the time, an office lacking independent budget or statutory authority would be incapable of overcoming congressional and bureaucratic resistance to any sweeping redistribution of authority and resources (*Logic*, 316). They were right, but the president was able to put off creating a new cabinet-level department until his staff could work out, in secret, a detailed plan for the department that satisfied the administration's ambitions. The result was a plan, unveiled on June 6, 2002, that was immediately recognized as the most far-reaching government reorganization since the formation of the Department of Defense after World War II (*Logic*, 290–291).

Homeland Security

The proposed Department of Homeland Security would combine twenty-two agencies with 170,000 employees and budgets totaling more than $33 billion, most taken from eight of the existing cabinet departments (Table 4). The main political battle was over personnel policy. The administration demanded the authority to write its own personnel rules for the department and, if it chose, to ignore protections currently enjoyed under collective bargaining agreements by the many unionized employees in affected agencies. Democrats, then in control of the Senate, balked at undercutting their union allies, delaying approval of the department until after the 2002 elections. Then, stung by Republican campaigns accusing them of sabotaging homeland security—several, including Max Cleland of Georgia, who had lost three limbs in Vietnam, were attacked in ads featuring footage of Bin Laden and Hussein—they relented and gave the president what he wanted: unprecedented, sweeping authority over the organization of a cabinet-level agency. As one political scientist observed at the time, "I think this president has done such a terrific job on focusing the American attention on terrorism. . . that

Table 4. Nearly Two Dozen Agencies Move to Homeland

AGENCY MOVED FROM	HOMELAND SECURITY DEPARTMENT			
	Border and Transportation Security	Emergency Preparedness and Response	Science and Technology	Information Analysis Infrastructure and Protection
JUSTICE	• Immigration and Naturalization Service • Office of Domestic Preparedness	• Domestic emergency support team • National Domestic Preparedness Office (FBI)		• National Infrastructure Protection Center
TREASURY	• U.S. Customs Service • Federal Law Enforcement Training Center			
AGRICULTURE			• Plum Island Animal Disease Center	
TRANSPORTATION	• Transportation Security Administration			
GSA	• Federal Protective Service			• Federal Computer Incident Response Center
HHS		• Chemical, biological, radiological and nuclear response assets		
ENERGY		• Nuclear incident response	• Lawrence Livermore National Laboratory • Environmental Measurements Laboratory	• National Infrastructure Simulation and Analysis Center • Energy Security Program
DEFENSE			• National Bio-Weapons Defense Analysis Center	• National Communications System
COMMERCE		• Integrated Hazard Information System		• Critical Infrastructure Assurance Office
INDEPENDENT AGENCIES		• Federal Emergency Management Agency		
OTHER	The Coast Guard (from Transportation), the Animal and Plant Health Inspection Service (from Agriculture) and Secret Service (from Treasury) report directly to the department secretary.			

Source: White House, reprinted in *CQ Weekly*, November 16, 2002, 3003.

Congress is essentially paralyzed." The Senate's most senior Democrat, Robert Byrd of West Virginia, put it in darker terms: "It is dangerous when a president believes that he supposes the people's consent to freely tamper with their liberties. It is even worse when we not only fail to impose restraint, but actually aid and abet the executive in a brazen power grab."[16]

The president had effectively taken the Democrat's idea of establishing a Homeland Security Department, used their reluctance to accept his version against them in the 2002 elections, and then used it to great advantage in the ceaseless struggle between the legislature and executive over control of the bureaucracy (*Logic,* 297–308). In wartime, the president's national security rationale for reducing transaction costs in managing homeland security policy trumped the Democratic Senate's normal reluctance to delegate broad authority to an agency whose leaders would be appointed and otherwise supervised by a Republican president.

Legislation establishing the Homeland Security Department was only a start. Its new secretary, Ridge, faced the daunting task of integrating its disparate elements—with incompatible bureaucratic cultures, personnel systems, computer systems, clienteles, and political relationships with Congress (*Logic*, 305–307)—into an institution capable of coping with the huge range of tasks needing coordinated attention if the United States were to be made secure from terrorists. The legislation provided for a year of transition to get the department up and running, but it was certain to take longer. Experts on mergers and acquisitions from the private sector—people who had overseen huge corporate acquisitions at General Electric, Hewlett Packard, and Lockheed Martin—were solicited for advice, for no one else had experience with reorganization on such a grand scale.[17]

The establishment of the Department of Homeland Security posed a major organizational challenge to Congress, too. Congressional and bureaucratic structures tend to mirror one another; when agencies are reshuffled, committee and subcommittee jurisdictions have to be reshuffled, too, or else agencies will find themselves reporting to more principals than they can accommodate (*Logic*, 219–220). Homeland security is so multifaceted that by one count, eighty-eight congressional committees and subcommittees, which included as members every senator and all but twenty representatives, held jurisdiction over one or more of its components.[18] Members of Congress relinquish jurisdiction over important matters with great reluctance, and homeland security was no exception. Outsiders (and a few insiders) advocated the creation of new committees in both houses to handle the new department's nominations, budget, and legislation and to oversee its operation. As one former deputy Defense secretary put it, "If they don't create a separate oversight committee in the House and Senate, there's never going to be a functioning department. You can't create a new department if all the elements of the new department keep going back to their old bosses."[19]

Some steps were gingerly taken in that direction in the House, which set up the Select Committee on Homeland Security, comprised of fifty Republicans and twenty-seven Democrats, most of them chairs or ranking members of panels that will have to relinquish jurisdiction if the committee is to do its job. Its purpose is to operate as a "one-stop shop" for the new department, coordinating the work of the regular committees and drawing on their expertise when required. But powerful committee leaders remained resistant, and not only out of self-interest. If a new committee took full jurisdiction over the department's component agencies, critics could plausibly argue the possible loss of the deep fund of experience and expertise (members' and staffs') within the component agencies overseen by their old committees. The result would be enfeebled congressional oversight.[20] The Senate made no immediate committee changes. Still, the problems posed by continuing jurisdictional confusion over the Department of Energy, similarly cobbled together to deal with the energy crisis of the early 1970s, stands as a negative object lesson, and the importance of homeland security will keep Congress under continuing

President Bush poses here with Homeland Security Director Tom Ridge (left) at an appearance to launch the Citizen Corps, a program designed to allow citizen participation in community Homeland Security activities.

pressure to put the collective good of jurisdictional coherence (reducing transaction costs) ahead of individual desires to hold onto politically valuable turf.

Bureaucratic Infighting

The wartime empowerment of the executive branch raises the stakes for bureaucratic competitors within it. Agencies with different missions, clienteles, skills, and ideologies compete for influence with the president, authority over policy, control of implementation, and resources. The most striking example from the Bush administration has been the infighting between the State Department, led by Colin Powell, and the Defense Department, led by Donald Rumsfeld, over guidance of policy toward Iraq. A newspaper account of this conflict reveals just how bitter it had become by the time the military phase of the Iraq war had concluded (see the excerpt "Diplomats on the Defensive").

Both the Department of State and the Department of Defense perform tasks integral to the conduct of U.S. foreign policy, but they have very different assignments. The State Department conducts diplomacy, managing the political relationships between the United States and other nations and international bodies. The Defense Department prepares to fight and win wars. Different organizational tasks generate different bureaucratic cultures (*Logic,* 305), increasing the likelihood of friction when each, in pursuing its tasks, makes the other's work more difficult. For example, the most effective course of military action may require ignoring the sensitivities of friendly or neutral foreign governments; conversely, maintaining international support for American foreign policy may require limiting military options and increasing risks to combatants. During the Bush administration, the endemic conflicts between the two departments have been intensified by ideological differences between the political appointees the president has chosen to lead them. These divisions became more acute when attention turned to Iraq after the Taliban regime in Afghanistan had fallen. Rumsfeld and his hawkish staff of defense intellectuals believed that removing Hussein's regime was essential to national security, and therefore the United States should use military force to achieve this end without delay, and, if necessary, without international backing. Powell's State Department was more cautious, more doubtful about the need for immediate action, and more concerned with developing international backing for the use of military force to overthrow Hussein.

In all such conflicts, the president ultimately decides who prevails. Diplomacy prevailed for a time. Powell and the president persuaded the UN Security Council to demand, under threat of war, that Iraq permit weapons inspectors to renew their investigations. Iraq's partial compliance was sufficient to keep the UN Security Council from authorizing the military action against Hussein's regime; among the countries opposed to using force were a number of nations usually considered the United States's closest friends: Canada, Chile, France, Germany, Mexico, and Turkey. When diplomacy failed, the president chose to make war on

Between the dramatis personae of bureaucratic politics—Secretary of State Colin Powell (far left) and Secretary of Defense Donald Rumsfeld (far right)—are the president and his two key assistants, National Security Adviser Condoleeza Rice and White House Chief of Staff Andrew Card. Rice and Card mediate department disputes and also help keep the president a safe distance from the combat.

Iraq, allied with a "coalition of the willing," of which only Great Britain supplied significant military resources.

Bush's decision to wage a preemptive war opposed by most of America's traditional allies represented a triumph for the civilian leadership of the Defense Department. The war's remarkably successful military phase (also, of course, a triumph for the uniformed services) sweetened the victory, as most of the immediate disasters predicted by the war's opponents—Iraq's use of chemical or biological weapons, the destruction of Iraqi oil fields, refugees by the millions, more terrorist attacks against the United States—failed to materialize. But a new struggle soon began over which institution would be in charge of reconstructing Iraq, which with the collapse of order, widespread looting, and incipient power struggles by competing Iraqi factions promised to be a formidable undertaking. The White House wanted flexibility in deciding which agencies would help rebuild Iraq and clearly favored a leading role for the Pentagon. However, many in Congress wanted the State Department, which traditionally handles foreign aid, to manage reconstruction funds. Jim Kolbe, the Republican chair of the Foreign Operations Subcommittee of the House Appropriations Committee, argued that the Defense Department should not get bogged down in "nation building," a task that would "degrade our armed forces' capacities to fight wars. The secretary of state is the appropriate manager of foreign assistance, and is so designated by law. Bottom line:

reconstruction is a civilian role."[21] Not incidentally, Congress would have greater control and oversight if reconstruction funds were treated as ordinary foreign aid. But once again, Congress deferred to the president on an Iraq-related issue, giving him discretion in deciding which agencies would spend the money.

Kolbe's doubts about a nation-building role for the armed forces were shared by many of its members. They are organized, equipped, and trained to fight wars, not to police cities, manage public works, or install democratic institutions. Thus they do not share their civilian bosses' ambition to control the process of rebuilding Iraq, a reminder that bureaucratic conflicts occur within as well as between agencies. Indeed, strong disagreements between civilian and military leaders in the Defense Department are routine. Rumsfeld had to overcome considerable resistance to develop a war-fighting strategy in Iraq that relied more on speed, technology, coordinated air support, and special forces units than on large numbers of heavily armed soldiers on the ground. The strategy's success will be used as a resource in future struggles between the civilian defense intellectuals around Rumsfeld, who want to restructure the military for twenty-first-century warfare as they envision it, and military professionals defending the force configurations and war-fighting doctrines that form part of their bureaucratic cultures.

The ascendancy of the Defense Department reflected, in part, wartime realities. But in the current period, it also reflects the president's own preferences. In wartime even more than in peacetime the president has the power to settle policy arguments among his appointees and their agencies; indeed, often only he can settle them. Since the terrorist attacks of September 11 gave George W. Bush's presidency its mission—defending the United States against terrorists and, by extension, anyone else who might threaten the U.S. homeland, directly or indirectly—the president has consistently proven more willing to risk action than inaction, more willing to alienate friendly nations than to accept the constraints of collective international action. It is not surprising, then, that influence over foreign policy has shifted from State to Defense.

Diplomats on the Defensive

Sonni Efron

Diplomats are paid to have cool minds and even cooler temperaments, but inside the State Department, plenty of America's elite diplomats are privately seething.

They are up in arms over what they see as the hijacking of foreign policymaking by the Pentagon and efforts to undercut their boss, Secretary of State Colin L. Powell.

"I just wake up in the morning and tell myself, 'There's been a military coup,' and then it all makes sense," said one veteran foreign service officer.

The first two years of the Bush administration have seen what the diplomat called a "tectonic shift" of decision-making power on foreign policy from State to the Defense Department, one that has seen the Pentagon become the dominant player on such key issues as Iraq, North Korea and Afghanistan.

"Why aren't eyebrows raised all over the United States that the secretary of Defense is pontificating about Syria?" the official, who declined to be identified, said, fuming.

"Can you imagine the Defense secretary after World War II telling the world how he was going to run Europe?" he added, noting it was Secretary of State George C. Marshall who delivered that seminal speech in 1947.

Leading conservatives and Pentagon officials say such comments show the State Department's failure to grasp how profoundly global politics and U.S. foreign policy interests have been redefined, especially in the aftermath of the Sept. 11 attacks.

President Bush's national security strategy calls for a forward-leaning, muscular foreign policy to prevent terrorists and "rogue" states from gaining access to weapons of mass destruction and to confront such threats, by military force if necessary, before they reach American shores.

"Anyone who thinks that you can conveniently separate foreign policy, diplomacy, national security and war-fighting is clueless about the realities of global affairs, power politics and modern" war, a senior Pentagon official said.

Neoconservatives argue that the Pentagon is ascendant because it has better internalized the president's worldview. The State Department, they say, has not succeeded in its main task of explaining U.S. policy to the world and winning support for it.

Pentagon officials stressed that they are cooperating with State, but the military's swift victories in Afghanistan and Iraq have boosted its stature. "When there is a track record of success, that tends to earn a heavier and heavier workload," the senior Pentagon official said.

In public, Powell and Defense Secretary Donald H. Rumsfeld have friendly relations, and their policy differences are cordial, if hard-argued. In private, Powell is said to roll his eyes at the volume of "Rummygrams" routinely sent his way that offer the Defense secretary's views on foreign policy.

However, at the day-to-day working level, mid-level State Department bureaucrats say they are alarmed by the ideological fervor of the Pentagon's civilian decision-makers and by how they leave State out of important decisions, brush aside the diplomats to get things done, or ignore tasks they do not want to perform.

After months of bitter battle over who should run postwar Iraq, the two departments finally agreed on L. Paul Bremer III, who was appointed Tuesday by Bush to be the top civilian administrator.

But in the larger ideological struggle, there is no compromise in sight. Diplomats interviewed for this story—all of whom insisted on anonymity because of the sensitivity of the political infighting—said they are profoundly worried about what they describe as the administration's arrogance or indifference to world public opinion, which they fear has wiped out, in less than two years, decades of effort to build goodwill toward the United States.

They cite as an example fallout from Iran being included in Bush's "axis of evil." Under the Clinton and Bush administrations, the State Department had been ordered to try to befriend Iranian moderates in order to counter that nation's Islamic fundamentalists. During the war in Afghanistan, American diplomats persuaded Tehran to allow U.S. military jets to fly over Iranian territory, a surprise foreign policy success.

However, within hours of Bush's State of the Union speech last year linking Iran, Iraq and North Korea as an "axis of evil," Tehran canceled U.S. overflight rights, according to two sources familiar with the negotiations. . . .

A mid-level official complained that intemperate remarks by administration hawks have damaged long-term American interests. "Goodwill is an element of national security—and perhaps one of the most profound elements of national security," he said.

The long-simmering interagency battle burst into the open. . . when former House Speaker Newt Gingrich, a close friend of Rumsfeld, accused the State Department of being "ineffective and incoherent" and of a near-treasonous failure to advance U.S. interests on the eve of the Iraq war.

Gingrich portrayed the foreign policy disputes within the administration as a clash of worldviews between a president focused on "facts, values and outcomes" and a State Department focused on "process, politeness and accommodation." Instead of taking advantage of the diplomatic momentum created by the Iraq war, "now the State Department is back at work pursuing policies that will clearly throw away all the fruits of hard-won victory," Gingrich charged.

Rumsfeld has said Gingrich was speaking only for himself. But the address and other attacks from neoconservatives are being viewed within the State Department as an effort to politically "decapitate" Powell.

Gingrich's speech triggered a bitter public response from the State Department. Powell noted during Senate testimony that diplomats are supposed to craft alliances and find diplomatic solutions. "That's what we do," he said. "We do it damn well, and I am not going to apologize to anyone."

In an interview with *USA Today*, Deputy Secretary of State Richard L. Armitage said sarcastically, "Mr. Gingrich is off his meds and out of therapy". . . .

Rumsfeld's dismissal of opposition among some allies to the Iraq war as the political weakness of "Old Europe" and other comments are cited by moderates in and out of government as having sabotaged Powell's efforts before the war to get a second United Nations resolution authorizing force against Iraq. A *New York Times* columnist recently dubbed Rumsfeld "the anti-diplomat," a moniker that has caught on in Washington.

Conservatives cite a long-standing situation within the department of what is often called "local-itis," the process by which foreign service officers come to identify and sympathize more closely with the countries in whose affairs they specialize than with American interests as defined by the sitting president. . . .

Many inside the Beltway regard the increasingly public rift between the agencies as just another in unending bureaucratic wars that mark life in Washington, but one that could damage U.S. interests if it encourages foreign countries to try to exploit the conflict. In South Korea, for example, many officials believe the North Korean leadership is more likely to miscalculate U.S. intentions because of the policy rift between administration hawks and doves. . . .

The current ideological spat "has nothing to do with whether U.S. interests are being defended and everything to do with trying to check a Pentagon run amok. It's the 'Dr. Strangelove' syndrome: There's very much the dominance by this institution whose sole role ultimately. . . is to kill people and blow things up and they do that very well". . . .

But what is widespread within the State Department is the view that the U.S. intervention in Iraq ultimately must be judged in part by whether it generates more anti-American terrorism. Diplomats worry that the administration is insensitive to the risks its policies carry.

"When I was a kid, conservatives were the ones who did not want to take big risks" to change the world, recalled one middle-aged veteran at State, adding that "these people seem willing to take huge risks" that can truly be termed radical. . . .

Powell remains highly popular within the State Department. But some wonder whether the former general is too loyal to Bush and should consider resigning if his powers are being usurped with presidential approval by the hawks agitating on his right flank. . . .

"If you've got to deal with the Pentagon at the working level, it's a difficult existence," one senior official conceded. "They're so ideological, and they're so over the top now that the testosterone is flowing" since the Iraq war.

"But morale here is not crashing," he said. "On the contrary, we are entering a period in which we are going to need to turn to diplomacy— in the Middle East and beyond."

Federal Judiciary

Inter arma silent leges (During war the laws are silent)
—A Roman legal maxim

It might at first glance seem surprising that going to war could dramatically disrupt the institutional standing of the judicial branch of government. After all, unlike the president and Congress, the judiciary has no constitutionally designated role in making war or conducting other foreign relations. Yet war invariably leads governments to take actions on matters that fall within the judiciary's purview. Soldiers are sent to war and resources requisitioned; numerous other sacrifices also, may be asked of citizens, some of whom will inevitably claim that the government has overstepped its authority and seek relief in court. During the Civil War, Secretary of War Edwin M. Stanton arrested or detained more than 13,000 civilians, in many instances on charges amounting to little more than opposition to the war. Even in an era before civil rights and liberties were a major judicial concern (*Logic,* 323–328), the Supreme Court was drawn into constitutional challenges to summary arrests and the suspension of habeas corpus.

War abroad also raises the specter of subversion, sabotage, and terrorism at home. When the Pacific fleet was decimated in the surprise attack on Pearl Harbor in December 1941, military planners feared that America's war industries, heavily concentrated in California and Washington state, would become Japan's next target. The following February, President Franklin Roosevelt used his executive authority to order all Japanese aliens and American citizens of Japanese descent removed from the West Coast and placed in internment camps. Again, a series of court challenges ensued.

A basic responsibility of courts in America's separation-of-powers system is to serve as referees, blowing the whistle when officers in the other government branches overstep their authority. Whenever the nation goes to war and the government takes extraordinary measures, people who are harmed by these measures naturally look to the federal courts for redress. But during wartime, judges have always found it difficult to second guess the executive and the military. In his concurring opinion in the Court's decision to uphold Roosevelt's relocation order, Justice Robert Jackson explained the Court's dilemma: "In the very nature of things, military decisions are not susceptible of intelligent judicial appraisal. They do not pretend to rest on evidence, but are made on information that often would not be admissible and on assumptions that could not be proved. . . . Hence courts can never have any real alternative to accepting the mere declaration of the authorities . . . that it was reasonably necessary from a military viewpoint."[22] A half-century later the Court could still be found conceding the judiciary's inherent incompetence to supervise actions taken in the name of national security, this instance in a 1999 immigration decision:

> The Executive should not have to disclose its "real" reasons for deeming nationals of a particular country a special threat—or indeed for simply wishing to antagonize a particular foreign country by focusing on that country's nationals—and even if it did disclose them a court would be ill equipped to determine their authenticity and utterly unable to assess their adequacy.23

These earlier cases help to account for the federal judiciary's current reluctance to take an active role in overseeing the war against terrorism. Although the American Civil Liberties Union and other "rights watch" groups issue weekly condemnations of administration policies they believe violate constitutionally guaranteed rights, the federal courts have so far declined to challenge the new regime of surveillance and prosecution policies erected since September 11.

In assessing the current state of civil liberties and the judiciary's role in shaping national security policy, it is essential to distinguish First Amendment liberties (freedom of speech, press, and religion) from those concerned with criminal rights (*Logic,* 167–174), including search and seizure (Fourth Amendment), self-incrimination (Fifth Amendment), and the right to counsel (Sixth Amendment). Expression and religion have remained as free as before, whereas the government has been permitted to "militarize" whole classes of criminal behavior and remove them from established "criminal rights" protections.

First Amendment Liberties

Shortly after the terrorist attacks in New York and Washington, personal freedoms appeared poised for retrenchment. Early public opinion polls showed respondents less protective of press criticism of the government's antiterrorist efforts and more willing to allow government monitoring of religious activities than before.[24] However, in contrast to past wars that gave rise to national censorship boards and other organized efforts to stifle dissent (*Logic,* 156–157), demands for conformity have been notably absent since September 11. Random acts of hostility and retribution, numbering in the hundreds, were directed toward people of apparent Middle Eastern descent, but President Bush and other prominent leaders quickly condemned these incidents, which were investigated by the FBI and upgraded to the special status of "hate" crimes. Within a month or so, such acts subsided sharply.

On another front, early airport screening of passengers in the aftermath of the attacks initially appeared to enlist racial profiling (*Logic*, 101–103). Indeed, the circumstances even gave rise to a national debate as to whether airport profiling of young Arab males was constitutional. By November the Department of Transportation had installed new airport screening procedures, which rejected racial profiling in principle although they allowed screeners to take language and speech into account as they observed boarding passengers.

Months later, as the Bush administration prepared for a military invasion of Iraq, the nation experienced its largest and most widespread antiwar demonstrations since the Vietnam War. Several demonstrations included more than 100,000 marchers. In late March 2003, groups in more than 2,400 communities across the country coordinated demonstrations opposing the impending attack on Iraq.[25] Some arrests were made, as was to be expected when tens of thousands of agitated individuals are cordoned off into limited space, but nothing resembling the bloody protests and police riots of the Vietnam era occurred.

Finally, the healthy condition of personal liberties was unwittingly confirmed by Attorney General John Ashcroft's announced plan to set up neighborhood spies—the Terrorism Information and Prevention System, or TIPS—among gov-

Probably the most newsworthy threat to free expression to arise during the past couple of years occurred when Stephen Downs (shown here at right with his T-shirt and his son Roger to his left) was arrested for refusing to remove his "Give Peace a Chance" T-shirt on the insistence of a security guard in a mall outside of Albany, New York. The action made headline news, where it was widely condemned by vigilant civil liberties groups and roundly ridiculed on late night talk shows. The charges were subsequently dropped.

ernment and private service workers (postal carriers, truckers, toll takers, and the like). The plan was greeted with derision on all fronts and quickly disappeared into the dustbin of ill-considered press releases.[26] Rights groups had a field day and promptly seized the issue for their fund-raising appeals. Postal and firefighters unions and even some local law enforcement agencies denounced the program as impractical, in part because they did not plan to participate. And in an increasingly rare display of bipartisanship, Congress quickly drafted an addition to the pending Homeland Security bill that explicitly prohibited any federal funds being spent on Ashcroft's scheme.

Summary of Major Provisions of the Patriot Act of 2001

Uniting and Strengthening America by Providing Appropriate Tools Required to Intercept and Obstruct Terrorism
PL 107-56

Title I: Enhancing Domestic Security against Terrorism

Authorizes and funds new counterterrorism efforts, acknowledges that the civil rights of all Americans should be protected, and modifies the International Emergency Powers Act to allow the president to confiscate property of those involved in attacks against the United States.

Title II: Enhanced Surveillance Procedures

Authorizes the sharing of surveillance acquired during criminal investigations with the intelligence community, expands permissible forms of surveillance, and authorizes the hiring of more translators to support counterterrorism investigations.

Title III: International Money Laundering Abatement and Anti-Terrorist Financing Act of 2001

Includes a variety of new financial regulations meant to help discover and prevent the laundering of money to support terrorist organizations. Specifies that Congress may pass a joint resolution placing a sunset on this provision for the beginning of FY 2005.

Title IV: Protecting the Border

Expands the number of personnel guarding the northern border of the United States. Directs the FBI to provide the State Department and the INS with criminal history extracts for processing entry and visa requests. Prohibits the immigration and permits the deportation of those with ties to terrorist groups or groups that endorse

Criminal Rights

In contrast to First Amendment rights, criminal rights protections have, since September 11, been sharply reduced for anyone suspected of involvement in terrorism. Curtailment began in the fall of 2001, when Congress enacted the USA-Patriot Act, a comprehensive law of some 900 provisions designed to ferret out domestic terrorists. Among its many provisions, summarized in the box, the Patriot Act relaxed constraints on surveillance activities, dismantled a formidable firewall separating criminal from domestic security investigations, and gave the government a freer hand in seizing suspects and their assets and in conducting

terrorist acts. Expands the foreign student monitoring program to various vocational schools and language training programs. Preserves and extends immigration benefits for victims of the September 11 attacks.

Title V: Removing Obstacles to Investigating Terrorism

Authorizes the issuance of rewards to help fight terrorism. Gives the FBI considerable leeway in accessing information in its terrorism investigations provided the investigations are not conducted entirely on the basis of activities protected by the First Amendment.

Title VI: Providing for Victims of Terrorism, Public Safety Officers, and Their Families

Expedites benefits for the families of victims of terrorism and public safety officers investigating or responding to acts of terrorism.

Title VII: Increased Information Sharing for Critical Infrastructure Protection

Provides funding for programs that promote information sharing among federal, state, and local law enforcement to prevent and investigate terrorist activity.

Title VIII: Strengthening the Criminal Laws against Terrorism

Defines terrorism and adds a variety of terrorism provisions to the federal criminal code.

Title IX: Improved Intelligence

Directs the intelligence community to work together and share information to fight terrorism.

Title X: Miscellaneous

Reaffirms the civil rights and liberties of all Americans, includes further provisions to fight money laundering, and authorizes studies on the feasibility of new security measures.

Civil Liberties v. National Security
Selected Post-9/11 Court Rulings

The Rights of Enemy Combatants
Al Odah v. United States   March 2003

Family members of twelve people being held as enemy combatants at a U.S. military base in Guantanamo, Cuba, brought suit seeking the prisoners' release, arguing that the detainees were noncombatants and were being wrongfully held. The U.S. Court of Appeals for the D.C. Circuit ruled that it lacked jurisdiction over the matter. The unanimous opinion, written by Judge A. Raymond Randolph stated that "aliens detained outside the sovereign territory of the United States" do not enjoy constitutional protections.

Padilla v. Rumsfeld   March 2003

Padilla, a U.S. citizen, was arrested for allegedly plotting a dirty bomb attack against the U.S. and was detained as an enemy combatant. Those petitioning on his behalf contested his being held under that status and requested access to a lawyer. Chief Judge Michael B. Mukasey of the U.S. District Court in Manhattan upheld the government's designation but ruled, against administration pressure, that Padilla should be allowed access to a lawyer.

Hamdi v. Rumsfeld   July 2002

Hamdi, a U.S. citizen, was arrested in Afghanistan and detained as an enemy combatant in a military prison in Norfolk, Virginia. Those petitioning on his behalf challenged his designation and sought access to a lawyer for him. The U.S. Court of Appeals for the Fourth Circuit reversed a prior ruling ordering Hamdi access to a lawyer. In remanding it for reconsideration, Chief Judge Harvie Wilkinson suggested that the trial judge give "considerable deference" to the government's concerns.

The Rights of Material Witnesses
In Re Grand Jury Material Witness Detention   April 2003

Hawash, an Arab-American, was detained as a material witness. An Oregon District Court judge ruled that he could not be held as such indefinitely.

U.S. v. Awadallah   April 2002

Awadallah, a community college student, was detained as a material witness in the 9/11 investigations. He continued to be detained while testifying before a grand jury and was charged with making false statements under oath. The United States District Court for the Southern District of New York ruled that material witnesses may not be held indefinitely and that the law only permits holding witnesses pretrial. As a result, the evidence gathered against him constituted an unlawful seizure under the Fourth Amendment and the charges against him were dismissed.

Closed Hearings
North Jersey Media Group Inc. v. Ashcroft   October 2002

Two New Jersey newspapers challenged the closure of deportation hearings to the media in Newark's Immigration Court. The Third Circuit U.S. Court of Appeals affirmed the government's authority to close all deportation hearings pertaining to national security. Chief Judge Edward Becker wrote in his opinion that because of the Attorney General's "experience (and our lack of experience) in this field, we will defer to his judgment."

Detroit Free Press v. Ashcroft   August 2002

This case weighs First Amendment rights against national security concerns. The *Detroit Free Press* argued for access to deportation hearings under the First Amendment after Chief Immigration Judge Michael Creppy issued a directive closing all "special interest" deportation hearings for reasons of national security. The Sixth Circuit U.S. Court of Appeals rejected the blanket closure and ruled that they must be determined on a case by case basis.

Release of Information
Center for National Security Studies v. U.S.   August 2002

In this case the Center for National Security Studies, the ACLU, and twenty-one other organizations sought the release of the names and other related details of all those being detained in connection with the government's investigation of 9/11 and related terrorist activity. The United States District Court for the District of Columbia ruled that the names of the detainees and those of their attorneys should be a matter of public record but that the government is justified in refusing to release details such as dates and location of arrest, detention, and release. The Court ruled that "the Government's asserted interest in withholding these particular categories of information greatly outweighs the public interest in obtaining it" under the First Amendment.

Search and Seizure
In Re Sealed Case No. 02-001   November 2002

This case involves the relaxing of wiretapping requirements for cases involving national security and whether evidence obtained in that manner can later be used in criminal proceedings even though it bypasses established search and seizure protections. The Foreign Intelligence Surveillance Court of Review, created especially for such issues under the Foreign Intelligence Surveillance Act, ruled that such surveillances, given the threat to national security, are reasonable and therefore constitutional.

Holy Land Foundation for Relief and Development v. Ashcroft   August 2002

This case challenges seizure of assets of designated terrorist organizations under the International Emergency Economic Powers Act as a violation of constitutional rights. The United States District Court for the District of Columbia most forcefully denied the Fourth Amendment claim, ruling that "Blocking orders are an important component of U.S. foreign policy, and the president's choice of this tool to combat terrorism is entitled to particular deference."

prosecutions and deportations. The implications of these changes for civil liberties and their potential for mischief were not lost on the legislators from both parties who drafted the legislation. These individuals were careful to include language prohibiting any use of this new authority against individuals exercising their First Amendment freedoms (for example, by expressing dissent or practicing a religion), and the lawmakers added sunset clauses specifying that many of the law's provisions would expire in 2005.

The Patriot Act eliminated routine judicial oversight over sensitive surveillance activities of law enforcement and intelligence agencies. No longer, for example, would a member of the FBI's criminal investigation division need to go to federal court to share information with a colleague in the FBI's domestic security division. Because the measure altered customary criminal procedures, its various provisions were bound to be tested in the courts. Judicial review of these new grants of authority continues, but as the summaries in the box "Civil Liberties v. National Security" indicate, so far the courts have supported the government's position in almost every instance. In part this reflects the judiciary's reluctance to meddle in national security matters. The Justice Department has encouraged the courts' abandonment of oversight by classifying many suspects as "enemy combatants" and claiming the authority to prosecute them in military rather than civilian courts.

Although some critics have concluded that the judiciary has proven yet again to be a weak defender of the Constitution against an expansive wartime executive,

Held beyond the jurisdiction of U.S. federal courts, prisoners captured in Afghanistan and transported to a military compound at Guantanamo, Cuba, have been denied defense counsel.

the relevant court decisions suggest a more complicated rebalancing of institutional authority among the branches. In virtually all the cases in the box "Civil Liberties v. National Security," government lawyers invoked one or more provisions of the Patriot Act, neither exclusively relying on nor sometimes even citing the president's inherent powers as commander in chief (*Logic*, 242–243). The availability of this public law allows the judiciary to cede authority to the executive more comfortably than if the administration were resting its case wholly on the president's commander-in-chief responsibilities during times of war. One reason is that public law certifies agreement between the two elective branches.[27] Moreover, statutory language is more specific and delimiting. The court is not asked to review the assertion of authority by one self-interested claimant, the president, based on the Constitution's general language. Any judge who accedes to an executive's novel interpretation of his inherent authority in a particular case has to ask, where does the authority end?[28] It is a question judges prefer to avoid, and reliance on the Patriot Act has allowed them to do so. In sum, the federal judiciary has so far largely acceded to broad claims of executive authority to fight terrorism, but less from recognition of its own incompetence in these matters than from accepting that Congress had, via the Patriot Act, legitimately delegated temporary and appropriately bounded authority to the president.

News Media

Students of American politics occasionally refer to the news media as the "fourth branch of government." They do so for good reason. The successful operation of a democracy is predicated on an informed citizenry. Without reliable information about the performance of elected officials, people would be at the mercy of the skewed, self-serving information supplied by those who wish to influence their votes and opinions. The Framers recognized that ambitious politicians might be tempted to monopolize, distort, or hide information, and so, to preserve the citizenry's control over its elected agents, they added to the Constitution the First Amendment, which unequivocally guarantees a free press, unfettered by government regulation.

Because news matters, politicians try to influence its content. Reporters in turn require information from politicians in order to produce their stories. Each needs something from the other—sympathetic coverage and reliable information, respectively—introducing the potential for reciprocity, even collusion. But reciprocal dependence can also lead to tension, mutual suspicion, and conflict, which in fact more accurately characterize normal relations between reporters and politicians. Politicians know that the best stories will sometimes be those told at their expense, and so they view reporters warily. Similarly, reporters know they risk losing their credibility and audience if they come to be regarded as flacks for politicians. The desire of each to exploit the other is rooted in their separate objectives,

The President as Top Gun

When President Bush landed on the aircraft carrier USS *Abraham Lincoln* to greet sailors returning from the Mideast, his arrival was chronicled by all the major broadcast and cable outlets and print media photographers. Widely proclaimed by admirers and critics alike as the "mother of all photo opportunities," cable news networks devoted the rest of the day's airtime to replaying the magnificently choreographed images. Even as most news outlets recognized it as a publicity stunt and characterized it as the unofficial launching of the president's reelection campaign, they could not conceal their wonderment. The *Washington Post* on May 2, 2003, marveled at "the bowlegged swagger of a top gun." Only about a third of the news sources, according to one analysis, echoed frustrated Democrats' criticism of the staged event.

Source: Global Media Analysts (www.carma.com/News/prweek/030519.asp).

fulfilling Madison's strategy of pitting "ambition against ambition," and fitting "the fourth branch" comfortably into the broader system of checks and balances. As President Bush's public relations coup described in the box "The President as Top Gun" makes clear, the competition between politicians and the press does not mean that the news will always represent a standoff; sometimes one or the other gets the upper hand.

A full primer on politician-press relations appears in Chapter 14 of *Logic*. We review the subject here because events since September 11 suggest that the discussion should be amended to include a set of participants whose political relations with the news media were not, until recently, so salient: military officers. After the wars in Afghanistan and Iraq, it is evident that relations between the military and the news media have acquired many of the characteristics of relations between politicians and the news media. This is not because soldiers have become politicians, although throughout American history some, indeed, have become politicians, but because until recently the military could aspire—although never with the expectation of complete success—to exercise monopoly control over the information that mattered. As long as the military could manage the news effectively, it was able to promote sympathetic coverage, bury bad news, and prevent useful information from falling into enemy hands. When a news reporter tried to acquit himself with the Union general William Tecumseh Sherman by saying that he simply sought to report the truth, the general instructed him to take the next train out of town. "The truth, eh? No sir! . . . We don't want the enemy any better informed than he is. Make no mistake about that train."[29]

The first Gulf war, in 1991, was probably the last war in which the military could hope to "contain" news reports from the front. Even then, the military found itself contending with network journalists in Baghdad filing independent reports about the accuracy of precision-bombing attacks and with other journalists breaking away from their assigned reporting pools and heading out into the desert unescorted in search of news (*Logic*, 503–505). It was the experience in Afghanistan, however, that convinced the military that it had to forge a new relationship with the news media. Advancing communications technology liberated journalists from transmission centers, removing them from military oversight. Hundreds of journalists roamed Afghanistan, unescorted and unconfined. At times, American soldiers found themselves approaching not the enemy but swarms of network and freelance reporters representing news media from all over the world. As one officer remembered ruefully, soon after a fire fight with the Taliban forces in a remote village, reporters from al Jazeera, the Arab television news network, showed up to conduct live interviews and transmit graphic images of victims while the American soldiers looked on.[30] As war approached in March 2003, hundreds, possibly thousands, of print and broadcast journalists descended on Iraq equipped with satellite phones and video transmission backpacks. Sherman's policy of banishing the news media from the front was simply no longer viable.

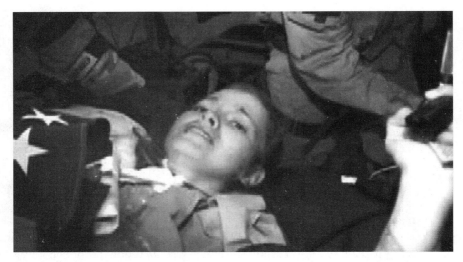

Seriously injured during a firefight, Private Jessica Lynch was captured by the Iraqi military and admitted to Sadaam Hussein Hospital. The POW's daring rescue reportedly required U.S. commandos to shoot their way into her ward. Revisiting the hospital weeks later, however, reporters heard a different story. Doctors and staff revealed that the Iraqi army had fled the day before and that the commandos were greeted at the gate by hospital staff and escorted to Lynch. A separate account even had sympathetic Iraqis driving Lynch to American ranks at one point, but turning back for fear that they might be mistaken for combatants. Was the news media hoodwinked by a military propaganda ploy? In an attempt to get the full story (or get the most out of it), media giant Viacom reputedly offered Lynch a lucrative package, which included primetime news interviews on its CBS subsidiary, a book deal with its publishing house Simon and Schuster, a spot on a musical video series on Viacom's cable channel MTV2, and, of course, a movie contract.

At the same time, the proliferation of twenty-four-hour all-news cable networks, with their insatiable appetite for fresh images, meant that the military could not simply ignore the problem. Communications technology in the field and news programming at home were combining to pull the public into the war as never before. The Pentagon's decision to take positive action was vindicated by audience numbers. A survey taken in early April, during the third week of the war, found that 95 percent of respondents claimed to be following the war closely. And nearly 70 percent stated that they were getting most of their news from one of the several all-news cable channels (FOX, CNN, and MSNBC).[31] As a consequence, public opinion closely tracked the war's daily progress. Between March 21, when it appeared that Saddam Hussein might have been killed in the initial bombing of Baghdad, and March 24, after a weekend of bad news, the share of survey respondents believing the war was "going well" plummeted from 71 to 38 percent.[32] Clearly, established procedures of pooling a limited number of reporters, controlling their travel, and feeding them carefully tailored information would no longer work. As one news editor summed up the military's emerging news dilemma: "[T]he Pentagon can't keep information from people, like it did so well in the first

A soldier, with an entourage of photographers, stands sentry during a sandstorm in the Kuwaiti desert south of Iraq.

Persian Gulf War. That's clearly going to be a losing game now."[33] Somehow, as they planned the war, the generals realized that they also needed a new plan for dealing with the news media.

"I'm a big fan" of the embedded press program, remarked Army general Tommy Franks, commander of U.S. forces in Iraq at one of his regular press conferences. He was referring to the military's new strategy of trying to get its version of the story out by persuading journalists to see the war the same way the military did. Specifically, more than six hundred journalists (as many as eight hundred, by one estimate) were assigned to military units. Within general guidelines requiring the withholding of information that might be useful to the Iraqi military commanders, who were reputed to be avid fans of America's cable news channels, reporters were free to interview soldiers and file reports from the field whenever they liked. Moreover, embedded slots were not limited to American journalists; even al Jazeera was awarded a half-dozen positions. Most assessments have concluded that the military's strategy was a brilliant stroke of political generalship. Just as the Pentagon had hoped, and some news editors had worried, the embedded journalists soon developed close personal relationships with their companions, and highly sympathetic stories of the American forces in action followed. In an attempt to balance coverage, the major networks and newspapers also hired "unilateralists," reporters who worked independently, filing stories from both sides of the front. (For a critical assessment of the quality of journalism that flowed from these new arrangements, see the excerpt "The Unseen War.")

Like General George Patton, Lt. General William Wallace rallies the troops for the sixteen-day blitzkrieg that would end with the fall of Baghdad. At other moments, however, Wallace behaved more like another famous general, Douglas McArthur, as he complained to the news media that civilian leaders in the Pentagon (i.e. Defense Secretary Rumsfeld) had sent his troops into the mission underprepared. Like McArthur, Wallace lost his commission.

Whether embedding represents a new equilibrium in military-press relations is difficult to say. The war was brief and highly successful. There were some indications that a tougher and longer war would have produced stories unacceptable to the top brass, however. It turned out that some of America's generals enjoyed candid on-camera interviews and did not hesitate to use their network appearances to disclaim responsibility for the failures, placing them instead on the secretary of defense's doorstep.[34] Moreover, the different military branches soon came to appreciate that favorable coverage from embedded journalists might strengthen their claims for a bigger slice of the Pentagon budget. As the war approached, the jostling for reporters and the media limelight became serious. By most accounts, the army was a big winner in numbers of both reporters and favorable stories filed with news bureaus. The navy attracted almost 150 embedded reporters, no small share of the total. But much to the chagrin of the admirals, the Pentagon instituted a news blackout as the ships launched their missile attacks. An undersecretary of defense tried to smooth over ruffled feelings: "The contributions of every service are going to be well known. We are a combined arms team nowadays."[35]

The Unseen War

Michael Massing

The Coalition Media Center, at the Saliyah military base in Doha, Qatar, seems designed to be as annoying and inconvenient as possible for reporters. To get there from the center of town, you have to take a half-hour ride through a baking, barren expanse of desert. At the gate, you have to submit your electronic equipment to a K-9 search, your bags to inspection, and your body to an X-ray scan. You then have to wait under the scorching sun for a military escort, who, after checking your credentials, takes you to the press bus. When the bus is full, you're driven the two hundred yards to the media center. The bus lets you off in a concrete courtyard surrounded by a seven-foot-high wall topped by barbed wire. If you stand on a ledge and look out, you'll see two rows of identical warehouse-like buildings. . . the offices of General Tommy Franks and the U.S. Central Command.

Journalists, though, never get inside these buildings, for they're restricted to the windowless media center, which is sixty feet long, brightly lit, and heavily air-conditioned. Inside the front door is a large space with long counters at which reporters for second-tier news organizations work. Extending out from this area are three corridors housing the offices of the TV networks, wire services, and major newspapers. Along the back wall is the door to the UK press office. Knock on it and moments later an officer in fatigues will appear and field your request. By contrast, the door to the U.S. office, to the right of the main entrance, opens onto an empty corridor, and if you knock on it no one will answer. Instead, you have to phone the office and leave your request with the officer on duty. If you're lucky, someone will come out and speak with you.

During the war, many of the reporters crammed into the center would dial the U.S. number, seeking to check facts, get some background information, or ferret out a bit of news. Usually, they'd be disappointed. Getting confirmation for even the most basic facts filed by reporters in the field would often prove difficult. Occasionally, a senior press officer would emerge to speak with a reporter, and within minutes a ravenous mob would surround him, desperately seeking to shake loose something even remotely newsworthy.

The daily briefings were even less helpful. Held in a large conference hall with the now-famous $250,000 stage set, the briefings were normally conducted by Vincent Brooks, a tall, erect, one-star general who is impeccably polite, unflappable, and remarkably uninformative. Each briefing would begin with a few choice videos. . . black-and-white clips of "precision-guided" missiles unfailingly hitting their targets, and color shots of American troops distributing aid to grateful Iraqis. No matter what was taking place inside Iraq, Brooks would insist that the coalition remained "on plan" and that morale remained "sky high." . . .

The Coalition Media Center is managed by Jim Wilkinson, a fresh-faced, thirty-two-year-old Texan and a protégé of Bush's adviser Karen Hughes. Wilkinson made his mark during the 2000 presidential election when he spoke on behalf of GOP activists protesting the Florida ballot recount. To run the media center in Doha, Wilkinson, a member of the naval reserve, appeared in the same beige fatigues as the career officers working under him. Nonetheless, the center had all the earmarks of a political campaign, with press officers always "on message." Many journalists, accustomed to the smoothly purring Bush political machine, were struck by the heavy-handedness of the Doha operation. A week into the war, journalists began writing their own "media pieces," as they called them, comparing the briefings to the infamous "Five O'Clock Follies" of the Vietnam War.

Rarely, though, did those stories examine how well the press, radio, and television themselves were doing, and that was unfortunate. For, with more than seven hundred registered journalists, the Coalition Media Center offered a superb opportunity for observing how reporters of different nations approached the war, and for understanding the many shortcomings in their coverage.

So stingy is Centcom with information that, at the daily briefings, the questions asked were often more revealing than the answers given. Those posed by European and Arab journalists tended to be more pointed and probing than those from the Americans. The Europeans and Arabs would ask about the accuracy of U.S. missiles, the use of weapons containing depleted uranium, the extent of civilian casualties. The Americans would ask questions such as: "Why hasn't Iraqi broadcasting been taken out?" "Is Iraq using weapons prohibited by the UN?" "Can you offer more details on the rescue of Jessica Lynch?" One U.S. network correspondent told me that she was worried that, if she pushed too hard at the briefings, she would no longer be called on. Jim Wilkinson was known to rebuke reporters whose copy he deemed insufficiently supportive of the war; he darkly warned one correspondent that he was on a "list" along with two other reporters at his paper.

After each briefing, correspondents for the major satellite networks would stand up in back and give a live report before a camera. Sometimes I took a seat nearby and listened. The British correspondents invariably included some analysis in their reports. After one briefing, for instance, James Forlong of Sky News observed that Tommy Franks had left the briefing to his "fourth in command" (i.e., Brooks), and that "very little detail had been provided." Referring to a question about a friendly-fire incident, Forlong noted that Brooks had little to say other than that the incident was "under investigation." CNN's Tom Mintier, by contrast, would faithfully recite Brooks's main points, often with signs of approval. "They showed some amazing footage of a raid on a palace," he said when introducing a clip that had been shown at the briefing, one of many that CNN aired.

Such differences in style were apparent in the broadcasts themselves. . . . [BBC] reporters were not afraid to challenge the coalition's claims. When an anchor asked Paul Adams, a BBC defense correspondent, whether Iraqi fighters were using "quasi-terrorist tactics"—a common Centcom charge— he said it was more appropriate to speak of "asymmetrical warfare," i.e., the use of unconventional tactics by forces that were badly outgunned. At the same time, the BBC presented many stories about the horrors of Saddam's rule. In one chilling piece, it had an interview with an Iraqi woman in London whose family members had been murdered, raped, or tortured by the regime. . . .

After watching the British reports, I found the American ones jarring. In my hotel, MSNBC always seemed to be on, and I was shocked by its mawkishness and breathless boosterism. Its anchors mostly recounted tales of American bravery and derring-do. After the U.S. attacks on the Palestine Hotel and the offices of al-Jazeera in Baghdad, MSNBC brought on its resident terrorism expert, Steve Emerson, who insisted before any of the facts were in that the attacks were accidental. MSNBC's "embedded" reporters, meanwhile, seemed utterly intoxicated by the war. In one tendentious account, Dr. Bob Arnot normally assigned to the health beat excitedly followed his cameraman into an unlighted building where two captured Iraqi fighters were being held near the entrance while a group of women and children could be seen in back. "They're fighting outside," Arnot said with indignation. "Here in the front are RPGs [rocket-propelled grenades] used to kill Marines, and in the back are these women and children civilian hostages. And they're terrified." But terrified of what? The captured men in the front room? The fighting outside? Were they being held against their will? Arnot never asked.

Before arriving in Doha, I had spent hours watching CNN back home, and I was sadly reminded of the network's steady decline in recent years. . . . [I]n Doha. . . [there] was CNN International, the edition broadcast to the world at large, and it was far more serious and informed than the American version.

The difference was not accidental. Six months before the war began, I was told, executives at CNN headquarters in Atlanta met regularly to plan separate broadcasts for America and the world. . . .

CNN International bore more resemblance to the BBC than to its domestic edition—a difference that showed just how market-driven were the tone and content of the broadcasts. For the most part, U.S. news organizations gave Americans the war they thought Americans wanted to see. . . .

Consider, for example, the day on which U.S. troops made their initial raid inside Baghdad. The fighting was so intense that, according to Centcom, between two thousand and three thousand Iraqi soldiers died. Yet, on TV, I didn't see a single one of them. On MSNBC, the anchor announced that its live video feed was being put on five-second delay so that images deemed too "disturbing" could be weeded out. On CNN the only casualty I saw was when Walter Rodgers and his crew found an Iraqi soldier lying wounded on the side of the road. A CNN security officer who had some medical training stopped to help the man while U.S. Army medics were summoned. This made for dramatic TV, and it showed the type of casualties CNN apparently thought appropriate for broadcast: those assisted by compassionate Americans.

Source: Michael Massing is a contributing editor to the *Columbia Journalism Review* and a frequent contributor to the *New York Review of Books.*

Conclusion

Since the terrorist attacks of September 11, 2001, the United States has been on a war footing. The Constitution's design gives the president primacy in defense matters, strengthening the hand of a wartime executive in dealings with other centers of power in government, notably Congress and the courts. The current president, George W. Bush, and his closest advisers held an expansive view of presidential prerogative even before September 11, and the administration has not hesitated to use its wartime leverage to expand executive authority wherever the opportunity has presented itself.[36] Backed by the widespread public support generated by his forceful and so far largely successful wartime leadership, Bush has been granted extraordinary deference in policy domains linked to national defense. Radical changes in national institutions (organization of the Homeland Security Department), defense policies (preemptive war in Iraq), and legal protections (the Patriot Act) have ensued. In circumstances in which the instinct of every politician, judge, and bureaucrat is to err on the side of too much rather than too little devotion to homeland security (better to be blamed for excessive security measures than for doing too little to prevent a new terrorist atrocity), opposition to the administration's aggressive defense and security policies has been muted and ineffective.

In other domains, however, politics as usual prevails. The widespread public approval of the president's performance and policies in the area of national security is not matched on the domestic side. Even after Republicans assumed full control of Congress in January 2003 Bush has had to bargain hard even for partial victories in the domestic arena. Members of Congress (particularly, but not exclusively, Democrats), reduced to unaccustomed deference on defense matters, have every reason to assert themselves on other fronts to restore some semblance of balance. The American people and their congressional representatives remain as sharply divided along partisan lines on domestic policy issues—taxes, Social Security, abortion, energy policy, and environmental protection—as they were before September 11. Wartime conditions have not made the president's positions on these issues any more popular than before, and they remain the stuff of normal political conflict among institutionally based partisans.

Once American military forces were in control of Iraq, domestic concerns reemerged. First and foremost among them was an economy growing too slowly to reverse the heavy job losses suffered since the Bush administration took office in 2001. For the 2004 elections, the president and his Republican allies will certainly try to make his wartime leadership, rather than the domestic economy, the defining issue.[37] Whether this strategy succeeds will depend on the continuing effectiveness of the administration's defense and security policies (maintaining order and stability in Iraq, prevention of domestic terrorist acts) and on an economic recovery strong enough for the president to avoid his father's fate (*Logic*, 400). The broader and longer-term legacy of institutional changes wrought by war and the continuing threat to homeland security remains obscure, but it is likely to shape American politics for years to come.

Acknowledgement: The authors would like to thank Laurie Rice for her diligent research and editorial assistance.

Notes

1. In the five CBS News / *New York Times* polls taken between October 2001 and January 2002 that asked the relevant question, from 87 to 89 percent of respondents approved of American military action in Afghanistan; it was approved by more than 80 percent of the Democrats as well as virtually all the Republicans. Bush's approval ratings on his conduct of the Afghan campaign were equally high.

2. See the comprehensive selection of polling data on the issue at www.pollingreport.com/iraq.htm, January 28, 2003.

3. In a Gallup Poll taken March 14–15, 2003, 51 percent of respondents said they thought that "Saddam Hussein was personally involved in the September 11th terrorist attacks," although no convincing evidence for this conclusion had yet emerged. After the fighting ended and American technicians were searching for the first unambiguous evidence that Iraq was hiding weapons of mass destruction, 81 percent believed that Iraq did possess them (CBS

News/*New York Times* poll of April 11–13, 2003, at www.cbsnews.com/htdocs/CBSNews_ polls/iraq_back0414.pdf), and 36 percent of the public believed they had already been found (NBC/*Wall Street Journal* poll of April 12–13, 2003, at www.msnbc.com/news/900352.asp# survey).

4. Indeed, some of them became less so. Gary C. Jacobson, "The Bush Presidency and the American Electorate," in *The George W. Bush Presidency: An Early Assessment,* ed. Fred I. Greenstein (Baltimore: Johns Hopkins University Press, forthcoming).

5. Results of various CBS/*New York Times* surveys, archived at www.pollingreport.com.

6. Gary C. Jacobson, "Terror, Terrain, and Turnout: Explaining the 2002 Midterm Election," *Political Science Quarterly* 118 (spring 2003): 1–22.

7. This broad antiterrorism package (PL 107-56), enacted at the behest of the administration, passed 357 to 66 in the House and 98 to 1 in the Senate during the last week of October.

8. Miles A. Pomper, "Senate Democrats in Disarray after Gephardt's Deal on Iraq," *CQ Weekly,* October 5, 2002.

9. Christopher Marquis, "Threats and Responses: Congressional Memo; Lawmakers Quibble over the Words of War," *New York Times,* September 26, 2002. Alison Mitchell and Carl Hulse, "Threats and Responses: The Vote; Congress Authorizes Bush to Use Force against Iraq, Creating a Broad Mandate," *New York Times,* October 11, 2002.

10. Kirk Victor, "Congress: Congress in Eclipse," *National Journal,* April 5, 2003.

11. Joseph J. Schatz, "Has Congress Given Bush Too Free a Spending Hand?" *CQ Weekly,* April 12, 2003, 858.

12. Niels C. Sorrells, "A Swelling Supplemental," *CQ Weekly,* April 12, 2003, 863.

13. Arguably, the figure understates the extent of the president's success. Even though less than half of the requested amount, the cut included most major provisions, at least in part. The tax on stock dividends, for example, was reduced to 15 percent rather than treated as ordinary income. And the ten-year projected reduction was lowered to levels acceptable to the administration by setting comparatively early expiration dates. In effect, the administration achieved much of its objective, but only temporarily and with each side realizing that the issues would be revisited over the next several years as expiration dates kicked in. Alan K. Ota, "Tax Cut Package Clears amid Bicameral Rancor," *CQ Weekly,* May 24, 2003, 1245.

14. Jonathan Allen, "Effective House Leadership Makes the Most of Majority,"*CQ Weekly,* March 29, 2003, 746–751.

15. Norman Ornstein, quoted in Niels C. Sorrells, "Lawmakers Not Eager to Revisit Iraq Supplemental Soon," *CQ Weekly,* April 19, 2003, 940.

16. Mary Dalrymple, "Homeland Security Department Another Victory for Administration," *CQ Weekly,* November 16, 2002, 3002.

17. Martin Kady II, "Security's Swelling Price Tag," *CQ Weekly,* January 11, 2003, 75.

18. Richard E. Cohen, Siobhan Gorman, and Sydney J. Freedberg Jr., "National Security: The Ultimate Turf War," *National Journal,* January 4, 2003.

19. Ibid.

20. Ibid.

21. Representative Jim Kolbe, quoted in Helen Fessenden and Jonathan Riehl, "White House Wins Flexibility in Planning for Postwar Iraq," *CQ Weekly,* April 12, 2003, 890–891.

22. *Korematsu v. United States,* 323 U.S. 223–224 (1944).

23. *Reno v. American-Arab Anti-Discrimination Committee,* 525 U.S. 471 (1999).

24. "Support of Free Speech Faltering, Poll Finds," *San Diego Union Tribune,* August 30, 2002.

25. Leslie Eaton, "On New York's Streets and Across the Nation, Protestors Speak Out," *New York Times,* March 23, 2003; Kate Zernike and Dean E. Murphy, "Antiwar Effort Emphasizes Civility over Confrontation," *New York Times,* March 29, 2003.

26. Dan Eggen, "Proposal to Enlist Citizen Spies Was Doomed from Start," *Washington Post,* November 24, 2002.

27. William H. Rehnquist, *All the Laws but One* (New York: Alfred A. Knopf, 1998), 218–225.

28. This conundrum was weighed in *New York Times v. United States,* 403 U.S. 713 (1971), where the Court turned aside President Nixon's assertion that his commander-in-chief authority allowed him to prevent press publication of classified documents without a strong national security justification.

29. Anecdote reported in Matthew Rose and John J. Fialka, "Even with More Play-by-Play, Truth Remains Elusive in Iraq," *Wall Street Journal,* March 31, 2003, A1.

30. Josh Getlin, "Public Would Get a Closer Look at War," *Los Angeles Times,* March 11, 2003.

31. Josh Getlin, "All-News Channels Find Big Audience," *Los Angeles Times,* April 5, 2003.

32. Rose and Fialka, "Even with More Play-by-Play."

33. Gitlin, "Public Would Get Closer Look at War."

34. Rick Atkinson, "Confused Start, Decisive End; Invasion Shaped by Miscues, Bold Risks and Unexpected Successes," *Washington Post,* April 13, 2003.

35. Christopher Cooper and David Cloud, "Military Branches Compete for Air Time and Credit: A Final Battle over Budgets," *Wall Street Journal,* March 26, 2003, B1.

36. Ronald Brownstein, "Bush Moves by Refusing to Budge," *Los Angeles Times,* March 2, 2003; Richard W. Stevenson, "President's 'Good' Guy Hurls Hardballs on Hill," *New York Times,* May 15, 2003.

37. Adam Clymer, "Buoyed by Resurgence, G.O.P. Strives for an Era of Dominance," *New York Times,* May 25, 2003; Edwin Chen, "Bush Cites War in Letter Seeking Campaign Funds," *Los Angeles Times,* May 25, 2003.